# Wildfire

HOUGHTON MIFFLIN COMPANY BOSTON 2006

Walter Lorraine *WL* Books

For Carter

www.houghtonmifflinbooks.com

Library of Congress Cataloging-in-Publication Data
Morrison, Taylor.
 Wildfire / Taylor Morrison.
    p. cm.
 ISBN-13: 978-0-618-50900-3
 ISBN-10: 0-618-50900-3
1. Wildfires—Juvenile literature. 2. Forest fires—Juvenile literature.
3. Wildfires—United States—Juvenile literature. 4. Forest fires—United
States—Juvenile literature.  I. Title.
 SD421.23.M67 2006
 634.9'618—dc22

                                        2005030483

Manufactured in China
SCP  10  9  8  7  6  5  4  3  2  1

# Wildfire

Taylor Morrison

Every summer huge forest fires burn in the West. The images, recorded on the television news, are similar: walls of flame twist into the sky, entire subdivisions are consumed. Newspaper headlines often read, "Killer Fires Must Be Stopped!" or "Fire Rages Through the Forest." Bright summer days darken behind thick smoke. The sky turns brown for hundreds of miles while flakes of ash fall like snow.

Armies of firefighters in yellow shirts appear. Fire engine lights flash and radios crackle as crews try to save homes in the fire's path. Grim-faced firefighters march out to the fire lines. Helicopter blades thump the air all day long while airplanes dump red fire-extinguishing chemicals. What are all those firefighters doing out there?

The people who work with wildfire are like lion tamers, attempting to control an extremely powerful and unpredictable force of nature. And as lion tamers do, they need to learn as much as they can about what they are trying to restrain.

In order to fight the wildfire, they must first understand how it works, and ponderosa pine forests provide important clues. How the plants and animals in this ecosystem survive and even depend on this seemingly fatal natural process gives researchers much-needed insight.

Thick bark protects the tree from the fire's heat.

Ponderosas drop their lower branches and flames cannot climb into their crowns and kill them. Many trees survive lightning strikes. They live because the long lightning scar doesn't circle around the trunk and girdle them.

Young pine saplings can resist fire when they are about six years old. Their long needles protect the buds from heat.

The native plants and animals in ponderosa pine forests need fire to exist, because it creates important parts of the ecosystem in which they live. The uneven patchwork of meadows, burned areas, and trees of various ages, all created by fire, provides food and shelter for a wide variety of life.

1. Bark beetles are attracted to old trees injured by fire. The insects burrow inside to lay their eggs. The larvae eat the tree's cambium while excavating tunnels.

2. Woodpeckers follow the beetle infestation. Lewis's woodpecker chisels through the bark to eat the larvae.

3. Rodents find seeds in burned areas, but they are often meals themselves. Fires clear out the forest's understory, so goshawks have a clear view and enough room to fly and hunt the rodents.

4. Elk and deer are attracted to the nutritious bunch grasses that thrive after a burn.

Many unusually intense forest fires have recently burned in the 80 million acres of ponderosa pine forest that cover the mountainous West and Southwest. Fire ecologists say that these unusually big fires show that the forests have become unhealthy because the frequent wildfires that used to naturally pass through them have not been allowed to burn over the last century. How can smoke and burnt trees be healthy for a forest?

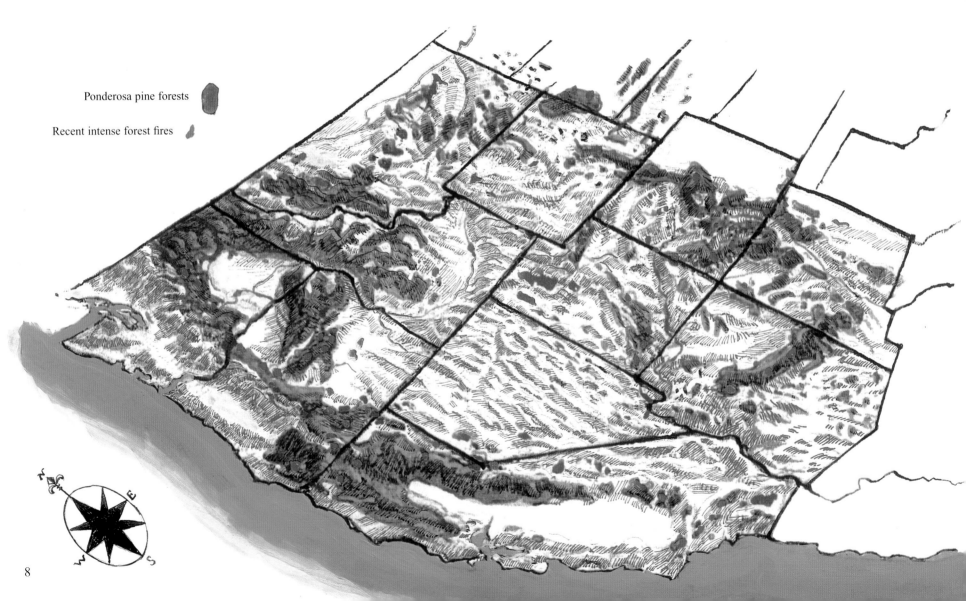

Ponderosa pine forests

Recent intense forest fires

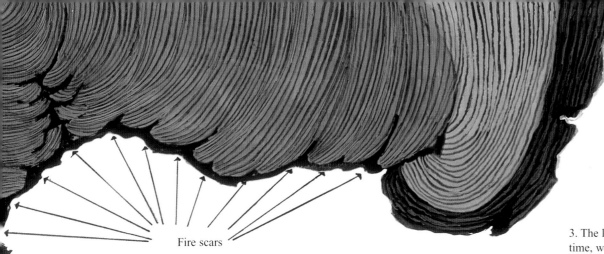

Fire scars

Some trees in these forests show that they have lived with fire for a long time. Scientists have counted as many as one hundred fire scars in the rings of ponderosa pine trees dating back a thousand years. The rings show each year of growth, and some reveal a black scar where the tree was repeatedly wounded by a fire.

1. Fire scars form on the side of the trunk away from the oncoming fire.

2. Sustained heating penetrates the bark and kills part of the cambium.

3. The living part of the cambium continues to grow over the wound. In time, wood curls over the edges of the wound. A large triangular scar, called a cat face, appears after many fires.

9

"Why are the fires so intense?" I ask a hot and tired firefighter. "The forests need to be cleaned up. There's too much fuel!" he explains. Trees and plants grow faster than they decay in dry western pine forests, so the forests naturally fill up with debris, just as smelly trash would fill up city streets without the regular return of the garbage truck. Fire removes and recycles all of the excess needles, brush, and logs, taking away the forest's garbage.

1. Lodgepole pine trees grow very fast and are densely packed together.

2. Lodgepoles live a short life, so this means that enormous amounts of dead trees pile up in the forest.

3. Lodgepoles avoid fire for about a century, until a stand-replacing fire burns.

1. Light amounts of clutter accumulate under large ponderosa pines.

2. A fire creeps along the forest floor, burning dry grasses and needles.

3. Branches, logs, and many young trees are burned up, but most of the bigger trees survive.

The basic pattern of how a forest burns is called a fire regime. A fire regime describes how intense and how frequent the fires usually are. Basically, the more excess forest debris there is to be cleaned up, the more intense the fire. In the past, ponderosa pines usually had small, frequent fires that cleaned up the forest floor like a vacuum cleaner. Lodgepole pine forests tended to have extremely intense stand-replacing fires that would kill vast numbers of trees about once a century. Some of the magnificent rain forests on the United States' northwest coast avoid fire for more than five hundred years, until a tremendous fire returns.

4. The fire kills giant patches of trees and melts resins in the pinecones, causing them to release their seeds.

5. Shortly after the fire, young lodgepoles, flowers, and grasses return.

6. The forest grows up until another big fire starts the process all over again.

4. The fire clears the soil and opens the forest's canopy, so seedlings get more sun and water.

5. Fires recycle nutrients by burning dead material. The ash from these fires enriches the soil.

6. Two to ten years later, another fire will arrive, maintaining the health of the large trees.

11

Land practices of the past have created large hurdles for today's firefighters. One hundred and fifty years ago the frequent fire regime of ponderosa forests was stopped. All across the West, sheep herders and cattlemen brought enormous herds into the meadows around ponderosa pine forests. The grazers ate so much grass that the surface fires lost the fuel that had always carried them. Additionally, loggers cut down too many big ponderosas, opening up unusually large spaces for little trees to grow.

The foresters who ran the U.S. Forest Service wanted to protect America's wood supply, so in 1935 they established a rule to extinguish all fires by ten a.m. the day after they started. Those in power did not want to consider the benefits of fire. Finally, in 1943, a brave forester named Harold Weaver published evidence explaining the harmful effects of eliminating fire from ponderosa pine forests. He saw that the forests were becoming sick and dangerously prone to big fires. But despite Weaver's discoveries, well-funded propaganda—including the popular image in poems and paintings of an endless pack of demonic fire wolves devouring the forest—convinced the public that all forest fires were evil.

Harold Weaver

Overgrazing

Excessive logging

Thicket of small trees

The effort to stamp out all wildfires made some forests unnaturally full of fuel. Once they do catch fire, these forests are dangerous for firefighters because all the extra fuel can make the fire explosive. A wildfire here must be found fast if there's to be any hope of controlling it. Airplanes and satellites can spot fires, but there is another way that has stood the test of time.

In the winter of 1910 a young forester named William Osborne worked on a surveying tool in his basement. Osborne emerged from his Portland, Oregon, home with a circular map attached to a sight. His invention was called a fire finder. The fire finders were placed in a network of lookout towers built on high peaks so fires could be spotted miles away.

Lookouts, who still perform this job today, live like hermits. All summer long they search for smoke from dawn to nightfall. Some cannot take the isolation: in one case a young lookout was stopped as he was about to jump off his tower because he thought he was Superman. One of the lookout's more dangerous jobs is to record how many lightning strikes hit the ground. Some of them describe metal objects glowing blue and their hair standing straight up as a thunderstorm approaches their tower. Lightning bolts have even exploded inside a few lookout towers. One man got knocked unconscious, woke up in a pile of broken glass, and then lost interest in the Forest Service.

William B. Osborne

14

Lookouts help firefighters on the ground by using their fire finders to find the exact location of smoke on a map. The lookout can swivel the instrument around 360 degrees, aiming it in any direction from the tower. The circular map on the fire finder covers 1,500 square miles of territory, with the tower in the center. Lookouts must memorize the terrain around them, because distances are very tricky to judge.

1. A lookout aims the fire finder at smoke and lines it up in the crosshairs.

2. Now the smoke must be somewhere along the line between the sights on the fire finder's map. To narrow the location further, the lookout reads the azimuth from the tower to the smoke off the outer ring of the fire finder.

3. A second lookout sights the smoke and reads a different azimuth off his fire finder.

Lookouts relay the shape, movement, and color of the smoke to firefighters in pursuit. White smoke with a wide base often means a fire is burning in grass, and a narrow blue or black puffing smoke could mean that heavy timber is on fire. Lookouts try to guide firefighters to within a quarter mile of the fire. They call in their observations by radio to a central dispatch center, and a dispatcher uses the sights of two or more towers to plot the location of the smoke on a giant wall map.

4. Dispatch center

5. Red circles on a wall map represent the lookouts. The dispatcher pulls strings out from the circles and lines them up on the degree of azimuth given from each tower. The intersection of the strings shows where the smoke is.

17

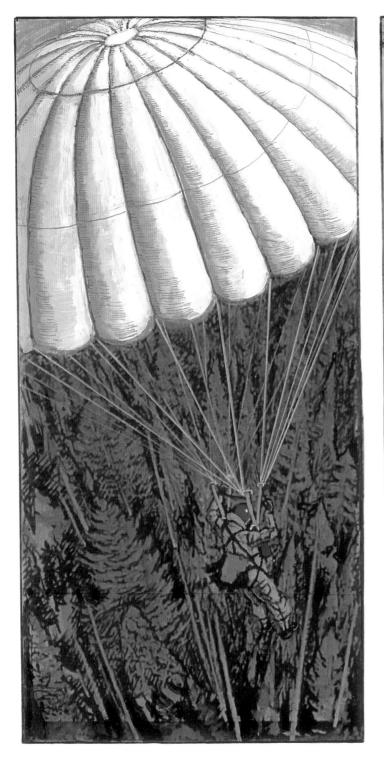

Dispatch sends out firefighters if human life, property, or a natural resource is threatened. Many fires are fought to protect timber, houses, or a watershed. The faster firefighters can get tools and water to a fire, the faster it can be controlled.

Fighting a small fire quickly is called "initial attack," and three daring methods of such firefighting involve the use of aircraft. In the first, firefighters called smoke-jumpers drop out of planes and parachute down to fires. They wear Kevlar jumpsuits because they often crash-land into trees. When they are finished fighting a fire, the smoke-jumpers carry out 110-pound back-packs full of their equipment for miles until they can be picked up.

Helitack crews rappel hundreds of feet down to the ground from helicopters, pursuing fire starts over millions of acres of land.

Retardant tanks

Water tank

Planes called air tankers drop a red chemical fertilizer called retardant onto fires to cool them down. The retardant is pumped out of large tanks into the planes at an air base. A person called a mix master prepares an exact amount of five parts water to one part retardant to control the weight of the liquid. Some of the larger tankers carry about ten tons of retardant. The mixture must weigh 9.1 pounds a gallon before it is pumped into the plane or it will be too heavy and cause the plane to crash. In the air, tanker pilots dive very low to dump a load. Occasionally firefighters on the ground are sprayed: a crew boss said that it feels like a shower of sticky syrup that penetrates your clothes and soaks your underwear.

The Neptune P2V is one of many World War II planes converted to fight forest fires. During the war it was flown over the ocean to hunt for submarines.

Engine crews are the main initial attack force of backcountry roads. The engines are portable warehouses full of chainsaws, digging tools, and a water pump. These pumps can push water through miles of hose. Firefighters use a progressive hose lay, a system of connected hoses, to quickly get water to a fire.

Initial attack is dangerous. A small wildfire creeping on the ground can suddenly leap into the trees and race off, or clouds of smoke may hide a wall of advancing flame. Still, only a tiny percentage of fires escape initial attack. If local firefighters are overwhelmed they call for more firefighters, engines, and aircraft to help.

Progressive hose lay

1. An engine crew heads to a fire.

2. They attach a hose from a hose pack to the engine pump.

3. One hundred feet of trunk hose unravels from the pack as a firefighter hikes to the fire.

4. A gated wye valve is attached to the end of the trunk hose. A new hose pack and hose are attached to the valve.

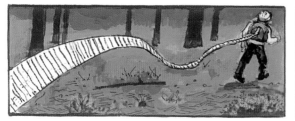

5. Water is brought farther and farther out as each new valve is attached and opened.

6. Firefighters spray water at the base of the flames to slow the fire down.

The calls for help eventually reach a giant base in Boise, Idaho, called the National Interagency Fire Center, or NIFC (*nif*-see). Sometimes thousands of homeowners must evacuate to escape big fires, which creates huge traffic jams. Many nervous evacuees demand of firefighters, "Save my house!" Some fires burn vegetation off hillsides, dislodging boulders and logs that can tumble down onto highways, squashing guardrails. Interstate highways, national parks, and forests are closed. When a wildfire wreaks havoc with civilization, NIFC helps control the chaos.

During the fire season the phones ring nonstop inside NIFC. The dispatchers shuffle firefighters and aircraft from Florida to Alaska, from California to Arizona, as plans change minute by minute. Overnight a city of tents pops up near a big fire. The fire camp is organized and supplied by NIFC. Food, power, medicine, tools, and water are provided for up to ten thousand firefighters. An incident command team runs the camp with a military chain of command. The teams have excelled at handling fires, so they have been sent to other emergencies like the Florida hurricanes, the crash of the shuttle *Columbia,* and the 9/11 terrorist attacks.

An anemometer records wind speed.

A wind vane records wind direction.

Remote automated weather stations, or RAW stations, collect information all year. There are nearly two thousand of them in the West. In Alaska, bears sometimes use them as jungle gyms.

On the edge of the forest fire the wind is blowing some plastic flagging west toward the fire. A few minutes later a firefighter says, "Did you see that?" The wind has shifted and the flagging is now blowing east, right toward us. I never would have noticed, but firefighters must watch for subtle hints that reveal what a fire will do next. Little things like a gusty breeze or the angle at which the sun is shining on a slope can lead to a blowup.

IMET presenting to incident command team.

The following illustrations show one weather pattern that can create a blowup.

1. Air from dense high pressure systems flows down into less dense low pressure areas.

2. In July the Northern Hemisphere is tilted toward the sun, receiving intense heat.

3. A high pressure system sits over the West during the summe[r] It creates clear, hot weather.

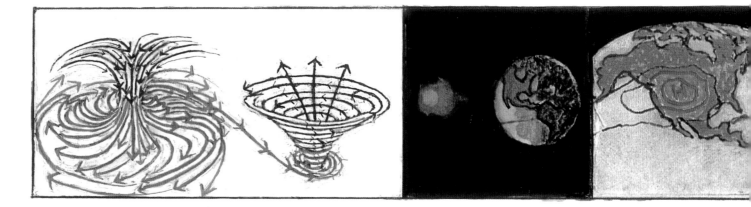

24

Working around a wildfire is dangerous. As one firefighter says, "As soon as you disrespect fire, it kills you." Superheated gases reaching 1600 degrees shoot ahead of a large fire front. Heat blasts have melted chainsaws and cracked boulders in half. The actions of air and wind strongly influence wildfire, but some of them cannot be felt or seen. Meteorologists help firefighters by forecasting the weather. They study the movement of air around the earth and then figure out how it will affect the local weather around a fire. The weather always changes, so meteorologists are constantly gathering information on wind speeds, air moisture, and temperature. Weather experts at NIFC even monitor how many lightning strikes hit the ground every day! They carefully watch the east side of the Cascade Mountains in Oregon and Washington. It is one of America's prime timber regions, where extreme fire danger persists. The winds are strong and the dry forests are overloaded with fuels.

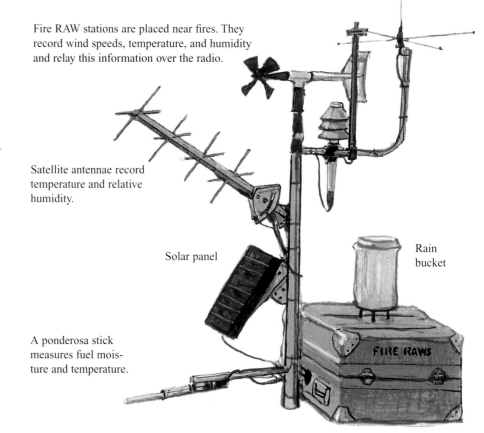

Fire RAW stations are placed near fires. They record wind speeds, temperature, and humidity and relay this information over the radio.

Satellite antennae record temperature and relative humidity.

Solar panel

Rain bucket

A ponderosa stick measures fuel moisture and temperature.

4. Gravity pulls down air in the high pressure system. It compresses and warms as it sinks to the ground.

5. The high pressure system pulls cool air off the Pacific. The cooler, heavier air runs into the Cascade Mountains.

6. It rains on the west side of the Cascades, but only dry, gusty winds make it to the east side.

7. Thunderstorms form on the east side of the Cascades. Dry lightning strikes a tree, igniting a fire.

8. The fire slowly backs down a slope in the afternoon.

Thousands of firefighters' lives often depend on a fire behavior analyst, or FBAN. The FBAN determines if it is safe enough for firefighters to work near a particular fire. They carefully study how the weather, topography, and fuels will govern it. Every fire is unique because these three elements can combine in an infinite variety of patterns.

Firefighters are always checking the relative humidity, the amount of moisture the air can hold when saturated compared to its actual state. When the air is saturated fuels are wet and don't burn as easily, like in the morning when dew forms on the grass. The hotter and drier the air becomes, the drier fuels get and the faster they burn. When the relative humidity drops very low, the stage is set for extreme fire danger.

Wet bulb

Dry bulb

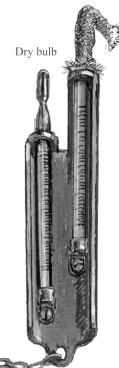

A sling psychrometer measures relative humidity. It has two thermometers: the dry bulb measures the actual air temperature, and the wet bulb, covered with a damp cloth, measures the dew point temperature. Then it is spun around, and the more water that evaporates off the wet bulb, the more it cools. The greater the temperature difference between the bulbs, the lower the relative humidity.

9. At night, cool air sinks into the valleys and pushes up a layer of warm air, creating an inversion.

10. The fire smolders in the morning moisture. Smoke cannot rise past the warm layer of air aloft.

11. The sun heats the slopes, making wind flow up the slopes, and the fire grows.

12. Moisture drops in the afternoon heat, and very hot air from the fire breaks through the warm layer.

13. The fire races uphill, creating so much heat that the smoke reaches into the cold heights.

When a fire blows up it releases as much energy as an atomic bomb every five to fifteen minutes. Some smoke plumes rise 40,000 feet into the atmosphere.

The powerful heat engine throws burning embers miles ahead of the main fire, where they ignite many new spot fires.

Tornados of flame called fire whirls form when strong winds create an eddy, or conversely moving current, around a plume. Fire whirls can rip trees out by the roots.

The fire sucks in oxygen, creating hurricane-speed winds. Branches and burning chunks are hurled upward.

Every morning there is a briefing at six a.m. to explain the daily strategy to the firefighters. All the experts funnel their information into a long plan, working on the thick document around the clock. In simple terms, the plan is to stop the fire from spreading by using dirt, water, and fire. It's like corralling a thunderstorm. Information officers translate and disperse the details about the fire to the media and the public.

A commander in the sky, called air attack, coordinates all of the aircraft. The air attack plane assigns missions and gives directions to the pilots while circling above them.

The water bucket on the Chinook can hold 2,680 gallons of water. A full bucket weighs 21,000 pounds.

Big fires cause a lot of air traffic. Giant helicopters retrieve and dump water all day long to slow the fire's progress. Some of the "heavies" create 100-mph winds that have blown trees down and sent small dogs flying through the air. Flying over hot fires is very risky. Burning embers hit the windshield as the pilots maneuver through the smoke. Heated air rising above a wildfire can shut the engines down or prevent the rotor blades from getting enough lift. Even the weight of the bucket can cause a crash if the bucket malfunctions and doesn't release the water.

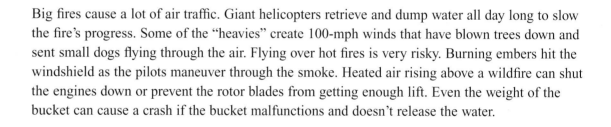

Water source

Sikorsky Sky Crane

Before charging into the forest, firefighters must be aware of a hundred things. They are constantly communicating and pinpointing the fire's edge to ensure that they are working safely. Field observers, aircraft, and satellites send in a steady flow of information to map the ever-changing wildfire. Special communication teams make sure that all the firefighters can talk to one another over their radios. They surround the fire with radio towers called repeaters, which carry radio waves over every hill and down into every valley.

In addition to thinking about their own safety, firefighters are mindful of the threat that their necessary firefighting machinery can have on the habitats of endangered animals. To keep the damage to a minimum, local experts called resource advisors alert firefighters to fragile places that can be harmed by bulldozers, helicopters, and fire.

GPS satellites relay the latitude and longitude of a fire line to dispatch centers. This information is then transmitted to firefighters.

Firefighters are careful when working around streams and spotted owl nests so that they don't damage them.

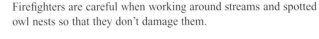

GPSs also guide the helicopters through smoke and to water dip sites.

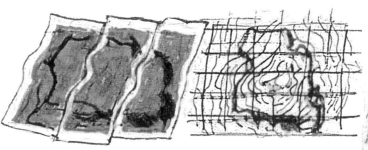

A plane flies over the fire with an infrared scanner that records the heat onto film. The film is given to an infrared interpreter, who draws the hot spots onto a map of the terrain.

Field observer

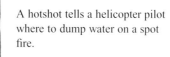

A hotshot tells a helicopter pilot where to dump water on a spot fire.

A repeater is hammered down with stakes.

Division supervisor

Even today, with all the amazing advancements in machinery and technology, most of firefighting is still tough, dirty manual labor. Firefighters hike into the wilderness where bulldozers cannot reach or are not allowed. Hand crews scrape out a trench called a fire line to block the fire's path. They dig down to mineral soil, which does not burn, so the fire cannot advance beyond it. Like football players, each firefighter has a position on the line. In front, sawyers with chainsaws carve a path through branches and logs, then swampers hurl the cuttings out of the way. Hunched over, following the blaring saws, are diggers in a long row. Someone yells, "Bump up!" to get the people in front to move forward. Each digger has a unique tool to chop, scoop, or rake his or her portion of the line. The most famous tool is a hoe and ax combination named after its inventor, Ed Pulaski, an Idaho forest ranger who saved his men from a firestorm in 1910.

Pulaski's bravery and loyalty embody the spirit of firefighters. They often describe feeling a strong bond of friendship with their fellow crew members. Chasing fires all over beautiful parts of the country is an exciting job, but many firefighters get homesick. Many of them can't remember a Fourth of July or summer spent with their families.

1. Sawyers

2. Swampers

Ed Pulaski

3. Pulaskis chop up the turf and cut roots.

4. Curved shovels called Reinharts dig up duff and soil.

5. Big rakes called Macleods are last in line, scraping away needles and leaves.

Firefighters light a burnout to remove fuel between the main fire and an anchor point. The anchor could be a fire line or a road. When the wind is blowing toward the main fire they light their drip torches and walk in parallel lines. Their torches drop flaming globs of gas onto the forest floor. Long strings of fire extend behind each firefighter until they merge into one big flame front.

Drip torches are filled with a mixture of four parts diesel to one part gasoline. The mixture pours out of a spout onto a lit wick and falls to the ground. The curve in the spout prevents fire from going back into the canister and exploding.

Cold trailing

Thousands of feet of hose are dragged.

The air smells like charcoal and smoke gently puffs up from the ground after a fire passes through. The silence is broken by the *crack-thump!* of a falling snag. Firefighters now begin mop-up, one of the dirtiest, slowest jobs imaginable. They line up side by side and march into the burned area, calling out "Smoke!" when they see something burning. They spend weeks crawling around in the dirt feeling for heat, which is called cold trailing. If they find hot embers, they scrape, stir, and soak them until the fire is out. As they work, hidden dangers are all around them: big stumps can burn underground, creating hidden sinkholes. Firefighters can get badly burned if they fall into one of these cauldrons.

Fighting fires is necessary at times, but it often comes with a high price. In 2002 more than $1.5 billion was spent on fighting wildfires. Also the chemicals used in firefighting, like retardant and foam, can harm the environment.

Instead of fighting fires, fuels managers use fire to restore the health of ponderosa pine forests that are overloaded with fuels. "The forest is encroaching on itself," explains a biologist in Arizona. At night in a dimly lit tent, a fuels manager sketches patterns of flame onto a map. Each pattern represents a different way that a fire could travel over the ground. He concentrates on how the southwest winds, the sloping plateau, and decreasing moisture would affect the fire. "I'm trying to get the flame lengths I want for the burn tomorrow," he says.

Months of planning go into figuring out when, where, and how to light a fire. Fuels managers must be extremely careful when adding flame to dry forests crammed with fuels and primed for explosive fires. Designing a prescribed fire is like balancing on a tightrope. The fire must not be too intense or it will kill big trees and destroy the homes of owls and goshawks in the canopy. On the other hand, it must be intense enough to burn up excess trees and brush. "Look at all of the gray and brown out there. All of that dead and downed wood needs to burn," says a fuels manager.

The next morning the burn boss instructs a lighter to start the first strip of flame along the fire line. The lighters walk back and forth through the smoke, laying down long lines of fire. The flames slowly creep downhill into the wind. The first strips are close together so the fire will have little room to burn and will stay small. A holding crew watches for any sparks jumping over the fire line.

Later on, the "good black" or burned line grows safely away from the fire line. The strips are spaced farther apart, making the fire grow bigger and bigger. Young pines and shade-loving fir trees are engulfed in flames. The fire opens up spaces so that ponderosa seedlings and native grasses will have plenty of sun and moisture to grow.

A large convection column rises above the fire. A helicopter flies in to extend the pattern of flame where the land is too vast for people to do this job on foot. Mounted on the door of the helicopter is a dispenser full of explosives the size and shape of Ping-Pong balls. The small plastic spheres are filled with powder. Thick metal needles inside the dispenser inject every ball with a liquid and then drop the balls to the ground. The liquid and powder mix until a chemical reaction causes the balls to burst into flames.

A ponderosa pine forest needs fire like an elk herd needs wolves. Wolves benefit the elk by controlling their numbers and preying on the sick, allowing the remaining elk to grow stronger and healthier. Fire does the same thing for forests, killing many small pines and weakening the old and sick ones. The strong surviving trees get more moisture and nutrients. A big, healthy ponderosa can defend itself against fire just as a strong elk can fight off predators.

Fire, insects, and disease are all part of a balance that has been controlling the number of trees for thousands of years. Taking away one of these simply increases the other two. Now fire use teams are trying to restore fire's natural process, but bringing wildfire back is not simple or easy to do. Around the Grand Canyon, across the East Cascade mountain range, in California, and all the way east to South Dakota are forests that need to burn. After being plugged up for almost a hundred years, many ponderosa forests are in serious need of prescribed fire so that they can return to their natural wildfire regime.

American Indians knew that wildfire was good for trees and that it controlled insects, and they regularly burned the forests. In 1854 a surveyor named Henry Abbott described how two Indians in California started a fire by rubbing a round stick against a block of cedar until sparks ignited the tinder underneath.

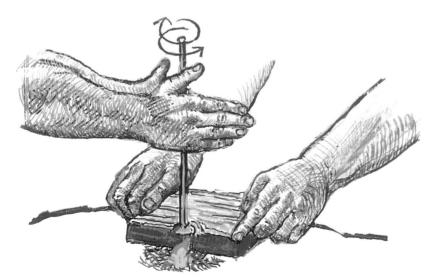

42

Early American explorers described enormous yellow trunks of ponderosa pines stretching out as far as the eye could see. Settlers easily rode their horses between the giant columns. The forest floor was covered with big patches of yellow, white, and purple wildflowers. Vast meadows of bunch grasses surrounded the forests. Bear, deer, and elk were abundant. Then loggers came in and fire was kept out, so the forest floor became cluttered with uncontrolled undergrowth.

Ponderosa pine forests can return to their former beauty with burning and thinning. However, prescribed fire is not popular: the public complains about smoke, and fuels managers are caught in a tight squeeze. When the air is stable it is safe to burn, but smoke from the prescribed fires fills the air. When the air is unstable, the smoke rises out of people's way, but the fire is more dangerous.

Today's explosive fires are a result of fire trying to catch up on its work, decomposing all of the fuels that have piled up. As one firefighter put it, "The forests are too cluttered—fires were stopped for too long!" And there is proof that prescribed burns do work: Several firefighters described seeing fires tearing through the treetops until they reached the site of an old prescribed burn. Then the crown fires appeared to slam into an invisible wall, plunge to the ground, and creep along the forest floor. Such evidence may help the people who work with wildfire with their biggest challenge: making the public accept fire as a natural process that can benefit people and the forest.

# ACKNOWLEDGMENTS

On a hot August day in 2003, brown smoke drifted over my house. Later on I found out that it came from a forest fire burning about two hundred miles away. While researching this book I used a sketchbook to draw what was happening on the fire lines during the day, and painted color studies from memory in my tent at night. One large firefighter saw me sketching him and said, "Son, what are you doing!" I was impressed with the people who managed the wildfires: they were generous, kind, and committed to educating the public about fire. They often displayed great patience while dealing with a wildfire, panicking evacuees, and an artist who kept showing up at their camp every day (at one fire camp I was called "the art puppy"). I hope this book does justice to their fascinating and important work.

More people helped than I have room to list, but I would like to thank a few to whom I am very grateful. Thank you to Chris Papen, Don Ferguson, George Broyles, and the rest of Pacific Northwest Team Three, who let me observe their work for two fire seasons. Jane Kapler Smith, Bob Mutch, Erik Christiansen, Warren Bielenberg, and Richard Bahr gave great criticism of my text and illustrations. David W. Tippets, Wayne A. Cook, Dick Bahr, and Jennie Albrinck arranged and allowed me to observe fire-use modules and prescribed fires in the north rim of the Grand Canyon. Rick Ochoa, John Saltenberger, Coleen Decker, Larry Van Bussum, and Bob Tobin explained how they do fire weather forecasts. Jeff Keener, Carson D. Watson, and Ann Mavencamp showed how repeaters are set up. Buddy Adams described the working of RAW stations in great detail. Amanda Burbank sent excellent photos of Edward Pulaski. Gary Morehead and Matt Hoehna showed me how engine crews work. Dave Robertson let me observe and explained a prescribed burn near Sisters, Oregon. Douglas S. Shinn and Christina M. Boehle explained what NIFC does. Jason Loomis let me participate in a week of firefighter training in Prineville, Oregon, and Rod Sams provided the required equipment. Bill Block, Brenda E. Strohmeyer, and Kristin Covert Bratland explained the process of fire ecology in ponderosa pine forests near Flagstaff, Arizona. Phil Armor and Diana VanCurler showed how things are done at the Redmond Air Tanker Base. Don Campbell and Ron George showed how the equipment is used in helitack. Bob Roth explained some advanced experimental technology used in firefighting. Dan Sweet arranged for a pilot to explain the workings of a Chinook helicopter. Lauri Turner described what a resource advisor does. Grant Kemp showed how firefighters and equipment are sent at the Central Oregon Dispatch Center. Ray Kresek gave a great tour at his amazing museum of firefighting history in Spokane, Washington. Vicky J. Kemp taught me the complex process of how the edge of a fire is mapped. John Ferrell located hard-to-find photos of Harold Weaver. Archivists at the Oregon Historical Society allowed me to make several copies of photos of William Osborne.

Finally, a big thank-you to my editor, Walter Lorraine, who remained supportive as this project grew longer than expected, and encouraged me to make the first draft of this book better.

# BIBLIOGRAPHY

Abbot, Henry L. *Explorations for a Railroad Route.* Washington: Beverley Tucker, 1857.

Agee, James K. *Fire Ecology of Pacific Northwest Forests.* Washington, D.C.: Island Press, 1993.

Boyd, Robert, ed. *Indians, Fire, and the Land in the Pacific Northwest.* Corvallis: Oregon State University Press, 1999.

Brown, James K., and Jane Kapler Smith, eds. *Wildland Fire in Ecosystems: Effects of Fire on Flora.* Fort Collins, Colo.: Rocky Mountain Research Station, 2000.

Butler, Ovid. *Rangers of the Shield.* Washington, D.C.: American Forestry Association, 1934.

Cottrell, William H. *The Book of Fire.* Missoula, Mont.: Mountain Press Publishing Company, 2004.

Kresek, Ray. *Fire Lookouts of the Northwest.* Spokane, Wash.: Historic Lookout Project, 1998.

Mutch, Robert W. *Forest Health in the Blue Mountains: A Management Strategy for Fire-Adapted Ecosystems.* Portland, Ore.: Pacific Northwest Research Station, 1993.

Newell, Marvin. *Firefighters' Guide.* Boise, Idaho: National Wildfire Coordinating Group, 1986.

Pyne, Steven J. *America's Fires: Management of Wildlands and Forests.* Durham, N.C.: Forest History Society, 1997.

————. *Fire in America: A Cultural History of Wildland and Rural Fire.* Seattle: University of Washington Press, 1982.

Reynolds, Richard T. *Management Recommendations for the Northern Goshawk in the Southwestern United States.* Fort Collins, Colo.: Rocky Mountain Forest and Range Experiment Station, 1992.

Schroeder, Mark, and Charles Buck. *Fire Weather.* Washington, D.C., 1970.

Smith, Jane Kapler, ed. *Wildland Fire in Ecosystems.* Fort Collins, Colo.: Rocky Mountain Research Station, 2000.

Smith, Jane Kapler, and Nancy E. McMurray. Fire works curriculum. Fort Collins, Colo., 2002.

Weaver, Harold. "Fire as an Ecological and Silvicultural Factor in the Ponderosa Pine Region of the Pacific Slope." *Journal of Forestry,* Jan. 1943: 7–14.

Whiteman, David C. *Mountain Meteorology Fundamentals and Applications.* New York: Oxford University Press, 2000.

# GLOSSARY

**AIR TANKER:** A fixed-wing aircraft that can transport and deliver fire-retardant solutions.

**ANEMOMETER:** An instrument designed to measure wind speed.

**AZIMUTH:** Direction from a point, measured in degrees clockwise from true north.

**BLOWUP:** The sudden increase in fire intensity or rate of spread, which usually makes it impossible to control a fire.

**BUCKET DROP:** Dropping of water or retardant from specially designed buckets slung below a helicopter.

**BURN BOSS:** The person responsible for supervising a prescribed fire from ignition through mop-up.

**CAMBIUM:** A layer of cells in the stems and roots of vascular plants that gives rise to the phloem and xylem.

**CONVECTION COLUMN:** The rising column of gases, smoke, and other debris produced by a fire.

**CREW:** An organized group of firefighters under the leadership of a crew boss or other official.

**CREW BOSS:** A person in charge of usually five to twenty firefighters, who is responsible for their performance, safety, and welfare.

**CROWN FIRE:** A fire that advances from treetop to treetop or along the tops of shrubs.

**DIP SITE:** Designated areas like a pond where helicopters refill their buckets with water.

**DISPATCHER:** A person who receives reports of discovery and status of fires, confirms location, and sends the people and equipment needed to control it.

**DIVISION SUPERVISOR:** A person who supervises the operations in a fire divided into different areas.

**DEW POINT:** Temperature to which a parcel of air must cool for saturation to occur.

**DUFF:** The partially decomposed organic material of the forest floor beneath the litter of freshly fallen twigs, needles, and leaves.

**ECOSYSTEM:** An interacting natural system including all of the organisms and environmental processes that affect them.

**FIELD OBSERVER:** A person responsible for collecting and reporting information about a fire from observations and interviews.

**FIRE ECOLOGIST:** A person who studies the effects of fire on living organisms and their environment.

**FIREFIGHTER:** Workers whose principal function is to put out fires.

**FIRE LINE:** The part of a control line that is scraped or dug to mineral soil. Sometimes called a fire trail.

**FIRE SCAR:** A wound caused by fire on a woody plant.

**FIRE SEASON:** The time of year during which fires are likely to occur and spread.

**FLAGGING:** Rolls of brightly colored plastic strips used to mark things like dangerous trees or escape routes.

**FOREST FIRE:** A wild land fire not prescribed for an area by an authorized plan.

**FOREST SERVICE:** An agency of the U.S. Department of Agriculture.

**FUEL:** Combustible material.

**GIRDLE:** To cut a girdle around a plant, killing it by stopping the flow of water and nutrients.

**GPS:** Global positioning system: twenty-four satellites that orbit the earth and provide instantaneous position, velocity, and time anywhere on the planet.

**HAND LINE:** Fire line dug by firefighters with hand tools.

**HELITACK:** A crew that uses helicopters to transport people, equipment, and retardant when a fire starts.

**HOTSHOT:** An intensely trained firefighter used mostly in hand line construction.

**INCIDENT COMMAND SYSTEM:** A standardized on-scene emergency management concept designed to allow people to use an organizational structure that grows and shrinks in proportion with the emergency.

**INFRARED:** A heat detection system used for finding and mapping hotspots.

**INVERSION:** An increase in temperature with height in the atmosphere. Usually the temperature decreases with height.

**NATIONAL INTERAGENCY FIRE CENTER:** A facility jointly operated by several federal agencies, dedicated to coordination of logistical support and improved weather services in support of fire management operations in the United States.

**PRESCRIBED FIRE:** The controlled application of fire to wild land fuels under specific conditions in order to confine a fire to a predetermined area.

**RAPPELLING:** Technique of landing from helicopters by sliding down on ropes, used by specifically trained firefighters.

**RELATIVE HUMIDITY:** The ratio of the amount of moisture in the air and the maximum amount of moisture that air would contain when saturated.

**RETARDANT:** A chemical that reduces the flammability of combustibles.

**SLING PSYCHROMETER:** A metal tool with two thermometers. After one bulb is covered with a wet cloth the tool is spun around, and the temperature difference between the bulbs is compared in tables to compute the relative humidity.

**SNAG:** A standing dead tree from which leaves and smaller branches have fallen.

**STAND-REPLACING FIRE:** An intense type of forest fire that kills vast patches of trees, usually in forests with infrequent fire regimes.

**TIMBER:** Growing trees or their wood.

**UNDERSTORY:** The plants of forest undergrowth.

**WILDFIRE:** Any fire occurring on a wild land, except a fire under prescription.